Sadlier

Review & Resource Book

Project Director
Kathleen Hendricks

Contributing Writer
Pamela Walker

Grade Five

Sadlier
A Division of William H. Sadlier, Inc.

Welcome to the **Grade 5 *We Believe* Review & Resource Book.**

The activities in this book are designed to be used with the core chapters in the Grade 5 *We Believe* textbook. The activities connect to the "Remember," "Key Words," "Reflect & Pray," and "Our Catholic Life" features found on the *We Respond in Faith* pages of these chapters.

Included are questions that will help you remember what has been learned, ideas for prayer and reflection, and suggestions for living the faith in everyday life. Some activities are suggested to be completed with a parent or other family member.

For additional ideas, activities, and opportunities:

Visit Sadlier's

www.WEBELIEVEweb.com

Nihil Obstat

✠ Most Reverend Robert C. Morlino

Imprimatur

✠ Most Reverend Robert C. Morlino
Bishop of Madison
April 29, 2004

Printed in the United States of America.

William H. Sadlier, Inc.
9 Pine Street
New York, NY 10005-1002

ISBN: 0-8215-5425-5
56789/09 08 07 06

Contents

CORE CHAPTERS

Jesus Shares God's Life with Us

Remember

John the Baptist, Jesus' cousin, preached about repentance and asked people to change their lives. He was preparing people for Jesus Christ, the Anointed One who would bring new life.

Imagine that you have been in a crowd listening to John talk about Jesus, and you have witnessed him baptizing people. Imagine that later you have a chance to see and listen to Jesus. Write about what you have seen and heard. Use these questions to guide you as you write about your experiences.

- What did John the Baptist say about Jesus?
- Why did John baptize people?
- What did you learn from Jesus?
- How did Jesus show you God's love?

Write the correct *Key Word* to complete each sentence.

Blessed Trinity
Jesus' mission
Kingdom of God
apostles
Church

- The ______________________ is the three Persons in one God.
- The power of God's love active in our lives and in the world is the ______________ ______________________.
- The ______________________ is all those who believe in Jesus Christ, have been baptized in him, and follow his teachings.
- ______________________ ______________________ is to share the life of God with all people and to save them from sin.
- The ______________________ continued Jesus' saving work when Jesus returned to his Father.

Reflect & Pray

Music is a meaningful and enjoyable way to raise our minds and hearts to God.

With a member of your family or group, make up gestures to go with the verses of the song, "Jesus Is with Us," found in your *We Believe* text. With a partner talk about what each verse means. Then together decide on clear and meaningful gestures to present the song in a new way. Use the space to describe what you will do and what each gesture means.

Our Catholic Life

The Kingdom of God grows when we:

- have faith in Jesus Christ and share our belief
- live as Jesus did and follow God's will for us
- seek to build a better community, a more just nation, and a peaceful world.

What are some ways you can "grow" the Kingdom of God? On each seed packet, write about or draw a specific way you can increase the power of God's life in the world and help the Kingdom of God grow.

Jesus Shares His Mission with the Church

Remember

The work, or mission, of the Church is to share the good news of Christ and to spread the Kingdom of God. We all share in the mission of the Church, and are called to proclaim the good news of Christ by what we say and do. How is the mission of the Church passed on from one person to the next, and from one generation to the next?

Jesus Christ described himself as the vine and us as the branches. We are joined to Jesus and to one another. On the leaves of the vine, write ways the mission can be passed from one person to another. The first few leaves are completed for you.

A father tells his son a story about Jesus and forgiveness.

The son makes up with a friend after an argument.

The friend does something nice for his little sister.

____
____
____

____
____
____

____
____
____

Across

1. ______ is the official public prayer of the Church.

5. Proclaiming the good news of Christ by what we say and do is ______.

6. Christ's passion, death, Resurrection from the dead, and Ascension into heaven is the ______ Mystery.

Down

2. Jesus Christ coming at the end of time to judge all people is called the last ______.

3. The ______ Works of Mercy are acts of love that help us care for the needs of people's hearts, minds, and souls.

4. The ______ Works of Mercy are acts of love that help us care for the physical and material needs of others.

1. 2. 3. 4. 5. 6.

FOOD DRIVE

Reflect & Pray

The Church prays the Liturgy of the Hours at different times during the day. In these prayers we celebrate God's work and his presence in our lives.

There are different ways to pray throughout the day. Think about special ways and reasons to celebrate God's work through prayer. Write a prayer that you might say at the beginning of the day.

Our Catholic Life

We give witness to Jesus when we perform the Works of Mercy. The Works of Mercy are acts of love that help us care for the needs of others.

With a family or class member, read over the Corporal and Spiritual Works of Mercy in your *We Believe* text. Together, write a plan that will help guide you to perform works of mercy. As you perform each one, place a checkmark next to it. Post your plan on the refrigerator or other place where you will see it each day.

Works of Mercy Plan

The Church Celebrates Seven Sacraments

Remember

The sacraments are seven celebrations that are special signs of God's love and presence. Jesus instituted, or began, the sacraments so that his saving work would continue for all time.

Sacraments are different from other signs in that they truly bring about what they represent. They are the most important celebrations of the Church, and join Catholics all over the world with one another.

Write a sentence about each sacrament, and place it under the correct sacramental group.

Christian Initiation

____

____

____

Healing

____

____

Service

____

____

Key Words

Complete the following paragraph by using the *Key Words*.

sanctifying grace
Christian initiation
common vocation
holiness
sacrament

A ______________________________
is an effective sign given to us by Jesus through which we share in God's life. This gift of sharing in God's life that we receive in the sacraments is called

______________________________.

All those who become a member of the Church by receiving the sacraments of

____

share a ______________________________,
the call to holiness and evangelization. Sharing in God's goodness and responding to his love by the way we live is

______________________________.

Reflect & Pray

The world is filled with signs of God's love. But Jesus Christ is the greatest sign of God's love. Everything that Jesus said or did pointed to God's love for us.

For the next few days, look for and write down signs of God's love. You may find signs in what people do or say. You may also find signs in nature. Keep your eyes and your heart open for signs of God's love. Write a thanksgiving litany or prayer and include each of these signs.

____
____
____
____
____
____
____
____
____

Our Catholic Life

The Holy Spirit helps us to be signs of Jesus. By continuing Jesus' work, the Church itself is a sign of God's love and care. Read the following scenarios with a member of your family or group. In the space next to each one, write how the people are being signs of Jesus. The first one is done for you.

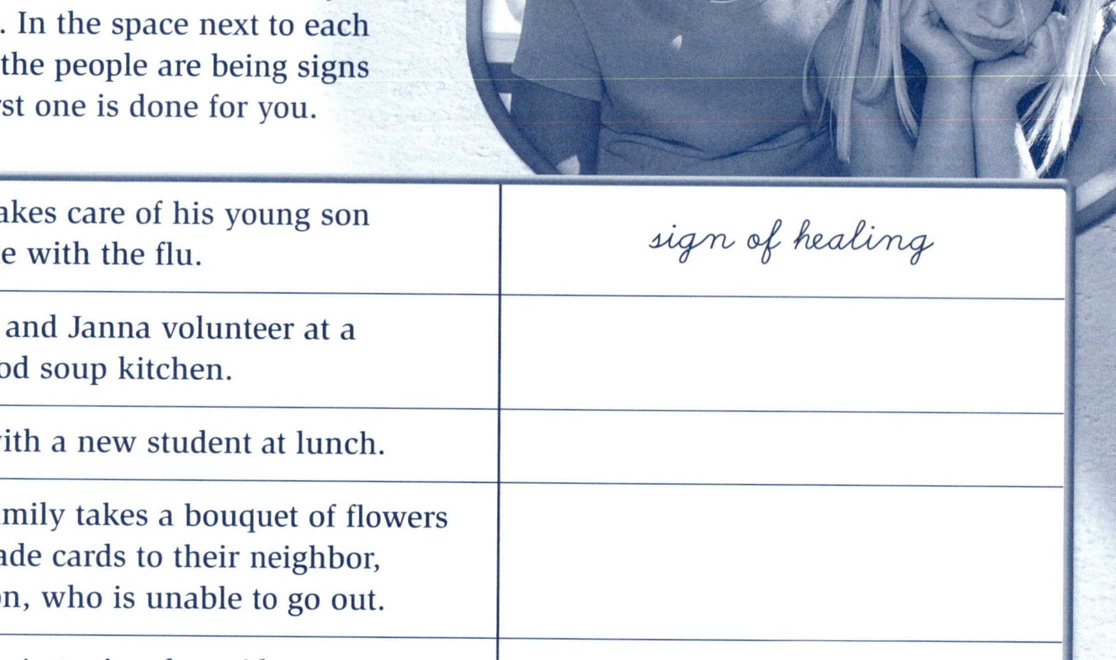

Mr. López takes care of his young son who is home with the flu.	*sign of healing*
Leesa, Tim, and Janna volunteer at a neighborhood soup kitchen.	
Pedro sits with a new student at lunch.	
The Luka family takes a bouquet of flowers and handmade cards to their neighbor, Mrs. Johnson, who is unable to go out.	
Ben forgives Antonio who said some unkind words to him in anger.	

What kind of sign or symbol would you design to represent each of the signs listed above? Draw some examples of these symbols.

New Life in Christ

Remember

Baptism is the foundation of Christian life. Jesus sent his apostles out to all nations to baptize believers. He wanted everyone to know him and to share his life and love.

How much do you know about the sacrament of Baptism? Take the following True or False Quiz. Circle the correct answer. Check your *We Believe* text to see how well you did. After you check your work, give yourself a "star" next to each correct answer.

☐	**True or False**	Baptism is the first sacrament that we celebrate.
☐	**True or False**	Baptism leads us to the other two sacraments of initiation, Confirmation and Reconciliation.
☐	**True or False**	In Baptism we are freed from sin and become children of God.
☐	**True or False**	Baptism makes us members of one family led by the parish priest.
☐	**True or False**	Through Baptism we are united with all others who have been confirmed.

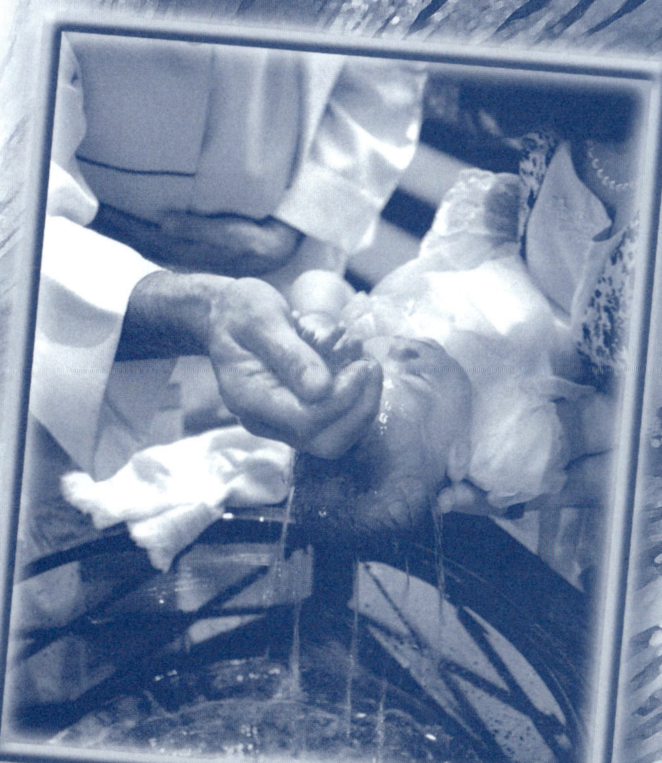

Unscramble the letters to make *Key Words.* Use them to complete the definitions.

hpertpo ____________

pmiBsat ____________

ntonicanraI ____________

rletaen fiel ____________

vnastloia ____________

isnsta ____________

The sacrament in which we are freed from sin, become children of God, and are welcomed into the Church is

____

The forgiveness of sins and the restoring of friendship with God is

____

Followers of Christ who lived lives of holiness on earth and now share in eternal life with God in heaven are

____

The truth that the Son of God became man is

____

Someone who speaks on behalf of God, defends the truth, and works for justice is

____

Living in happiness with God forever is

____

Reflect & Pray

Read the Scripture passage from "We Gather in Prayer" page in your *We Believe* text.

Illustrate the words from the book of Isaiah. Then with a member of your family or group, think of a way to incorporate the reading into a dramatic skit or interpretive movement. Write about it in the space below your picture.

Our Catholic Life

We share in Jesus' role of priest, prophet, and king. Think about what it means to share these roles with Jesus. How could a fifth grader live out these roles?

Write a story about a boy or girl who lives out the three roles of priest, prophet, and king, within the course of a single day. Make your character believable and his or her situation real so that your readers can relate to your story.

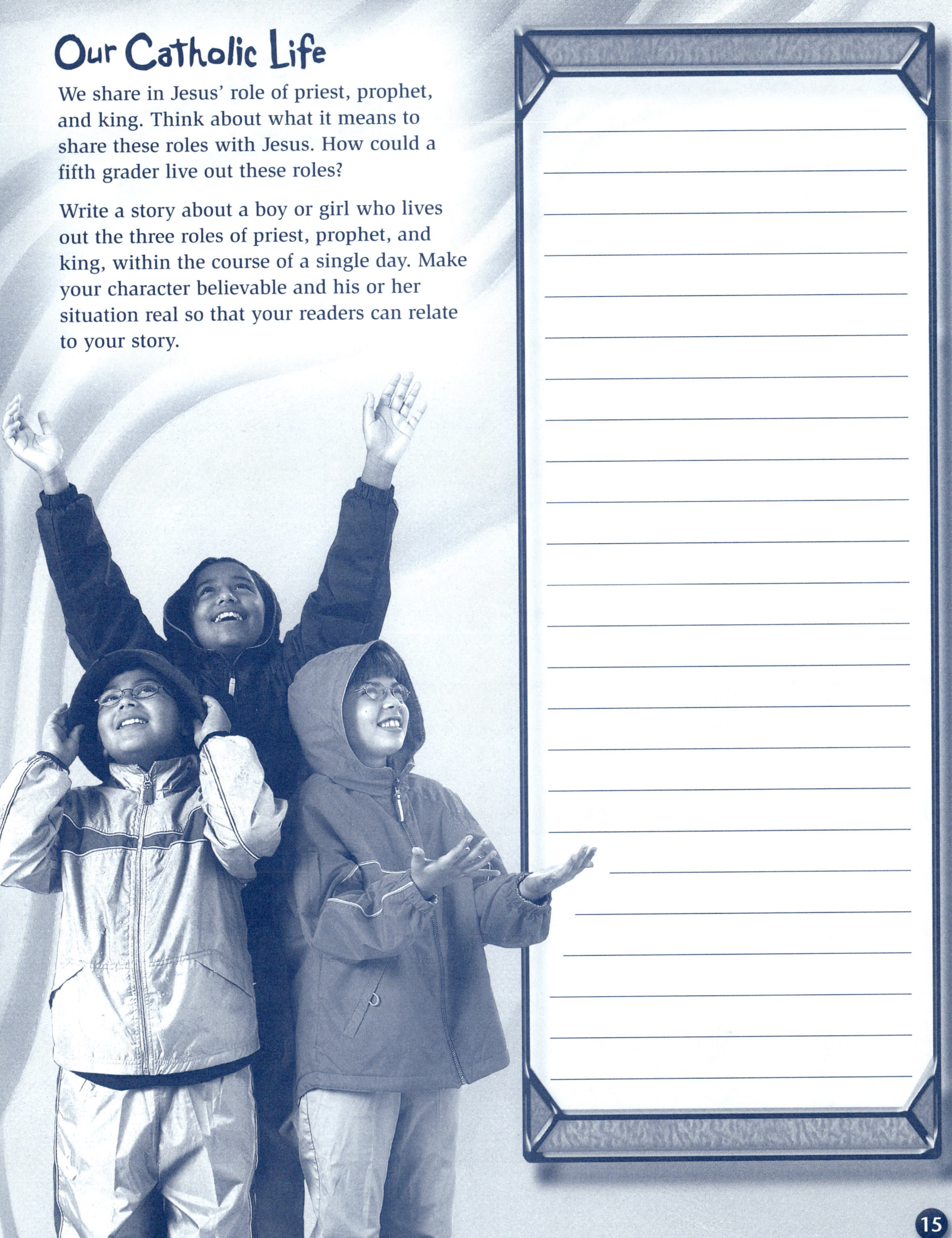

The Celebration of Baptism

Remember

The Church welcomes all to be baptized. The parish community participates in this celebration.

Read the caption below each box. Illustrate each part of the baptismal rite for children.

The celebrant greets the family, and the parents and godparents present the child to the Church for Baptism.

The celebrant traces the sign of the cross on the child's forehead and invites the parents and godparents to do the same.

The celebrant then prays asking God to free the child from original sin. He calls upon God for help and support and touches the water with his right hand.

The celebrant asks the parents and godparents some questions. They state what they believe.

The celebrant can immerse the child in water three times, or can pour water over the child three times.

The celebrant anoints the newly baptized on the crown of the head with chrism.

Key Words

Read the following statements about each of the *Key Words*. Circle the statements that are **True**. Draw a line through the statements that are **False**.

The catechumenate is a period of formation for Christian initiation. It includes prayer and liturgy, religious instruction, and service to others. Those who enter this formation are called the newly baptized.

Chrism is water that has been blessed by the bishop. The celebrant anoints the newly baptized on the crown of the head with chrism. This anointing is a sign of the gift of the parish.

Reflect & Pray

Water is an important sign of Baptism. In the sacrament of Baptism, the water is blessed with a prayer in which we recall that water has been a source of holiness, freedom, and new life.

Name one way we use water in our daily life:

- in our homes

  ____

- in our neighborhoods

  ____

- in our parks and recreation areas

  ____

- in our energy plants

  ____

- in schools and businesses.

  ____

Write a prayer of thanksgiving for God's gift of water.

____

____

____

____

____

____

____

____

____

Our Catholic Life

How does it feel to be welcomed? What are some ways you can make others feel welcome at your parish, school, on a team, or in a special activity in which you are involved?

Use the space to design a decorative card and write a letter to an adult catechumen and to a child who are both going to be baptized.

The Coming of the Holy Spirit

CHAPTER 8 REVIEW & RESOURCE

Remember

After his Resurrection, Jesus sent his apostles to preach in his name and to baptize those who believed in him. He promised to send the Holy Spirit to guide and help them. It was on Pentecost that the Holy Spirit came upon the first disciples.

Use the first two spaces to make digital "photos" showing the Spirit coming to the disciples and Peter preaching to the crowds.

Write a brief caption telling what is happening in each picture. In the third box, draw a picture that shows how we celebrate the feast of Pentecost today.

Reflect & Pray

When the apostles placed their hands on the newly baptized, they received the strengthening power of the Holy Spirit. This laying on of hands was a sign of God's blessing. The anointing that took place with the laying on of hands was a sign of the Holy Spirit's presence and of the receiving of the Holy Spirit. Today in the sacrament of Confirmation, the anointing with oil is done as the celebrant lays his hands on the head of the one being confirmed.

Talk with a family member or friend about the daily struggles a new believer at the first Pentecost might have had to face. Compare these to struggles that a newly confirmed person faces today. How are they both strengthened by the laying on of hands and the anointing with oil? Write a prayer of thanksgiving for this strength we receive in the sacrament of Confirmation.

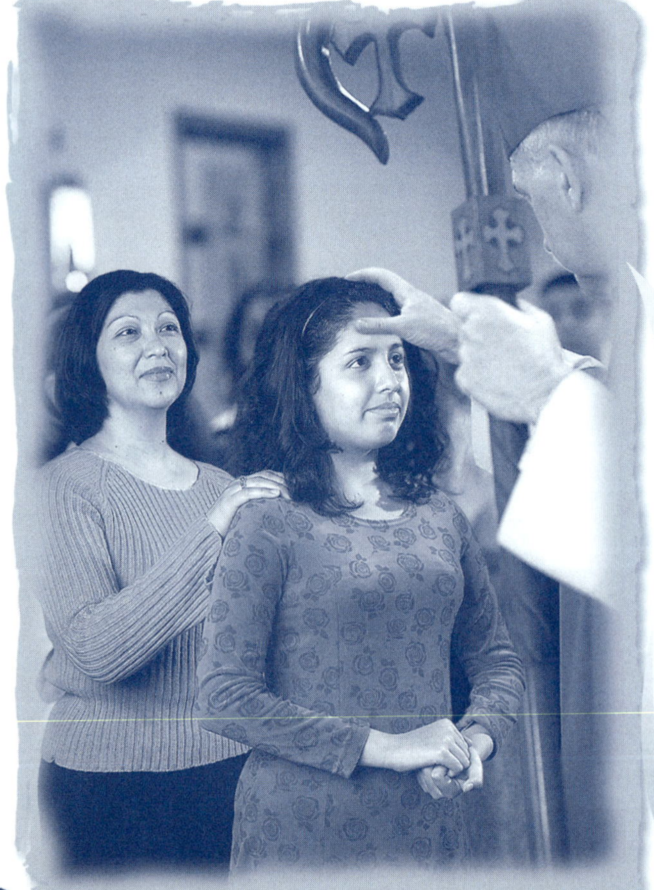

In the sacrament of Confirmation we receive the Gift of the Holy Spirit in a special way. We become more like Christ and are strengthened to be his witnesses.

Using the letters in the word *Confirmation*, write a sentence that tells something you know about this sacrament. The first one has been done for you.

It is a sacrament of **C**hristian initiation.

______________ **O** ______________

______________ **N** ______________

______________ **F** ______________

______________ **I** ______________

______________ **R** ______________

______________ **M** ______________

______________ **A** ______________

______________ **T** ______________

______________ **I** ______________

______________ **O** ______________

______________ **N** ______________

Our Catholic Life

God the Holy Spirit is always with the Church. We can turn to the Holy Spirit for comfort, guidance, and strength.

Write a note to a young person preparing for Confirmation. Tell some specific ways he or she may find comfort, guidance, and strength offered by the Holy Spirit. For example, when faced with making a tough decision, how might he or she be guided by the Holy Spirit? Be specific so this young person will understand how becoming more like Christ will help in his or her daily life.

The Celebration of Confirmation

Remember

Confirmation is the second sacrament of initiation. It seals us with the Gift of the Holy Spirit and continues the life of grace we first received at Baptism. Listed below are some of the steps in the Confirmation rite, but they are out of order. Using numbers 1–8 place the steps in the correct order.

The bishop confirms each candidate by the anointing of chrism on the forehead.	
The bishop shares a sign of peace with the newly confirmed.	
The candidates stand and renew their baptismal promises.	
The pastor or a parish leader presents those to be confirmed.	
The whole Church prays for all these candidates.	
The sponsor stands near the candidate and places a hand on the candidate's shoulder.	
The newly confirmed join with all assembled to continue to worship God by sharing in the gift of Jesus in the Eucharist.	
The bishop and priests celebrating with him extend their hands over the whole group of candidates.	

When we receive the sacrament of Confirmation, the Holy Spirit strengthens us with special gifts. These seven gifts of the Holy Spirit help us to live as faithful followers of Jesus Christ.

Draw a picture to show, and write a sentence to tell a way the seven gifts help you to live as a disciple of Jesus.

GUIDE

Helper

GIFT

Reflect & Pray

God continually blesses us with many gifts. Because God first blessed us, we, too, can pray for his blessings on people and things.

What sort of blessing would you ask for someone who is preparing for Confirmation? Write your prayer, and then work with a partner to combine your prayers. Come up with one prayer that you can send to a Confirmation candidate.

Our Catholic Life

An advocate is someone who intercedes on our behalf, speaks for us, or even defends us. An advocate comforts and teaches.

How can the Holy Spirit be an advocate for a fifth grader? Write a two-person skit that describes various situations when a fifth grader would want and/or need an advocate. Then with a member of your group, act out the skit, taking turns playing the part of the fifth grader who describes the situation, and the part of the advocate who intercedes, comforts, and teaches.

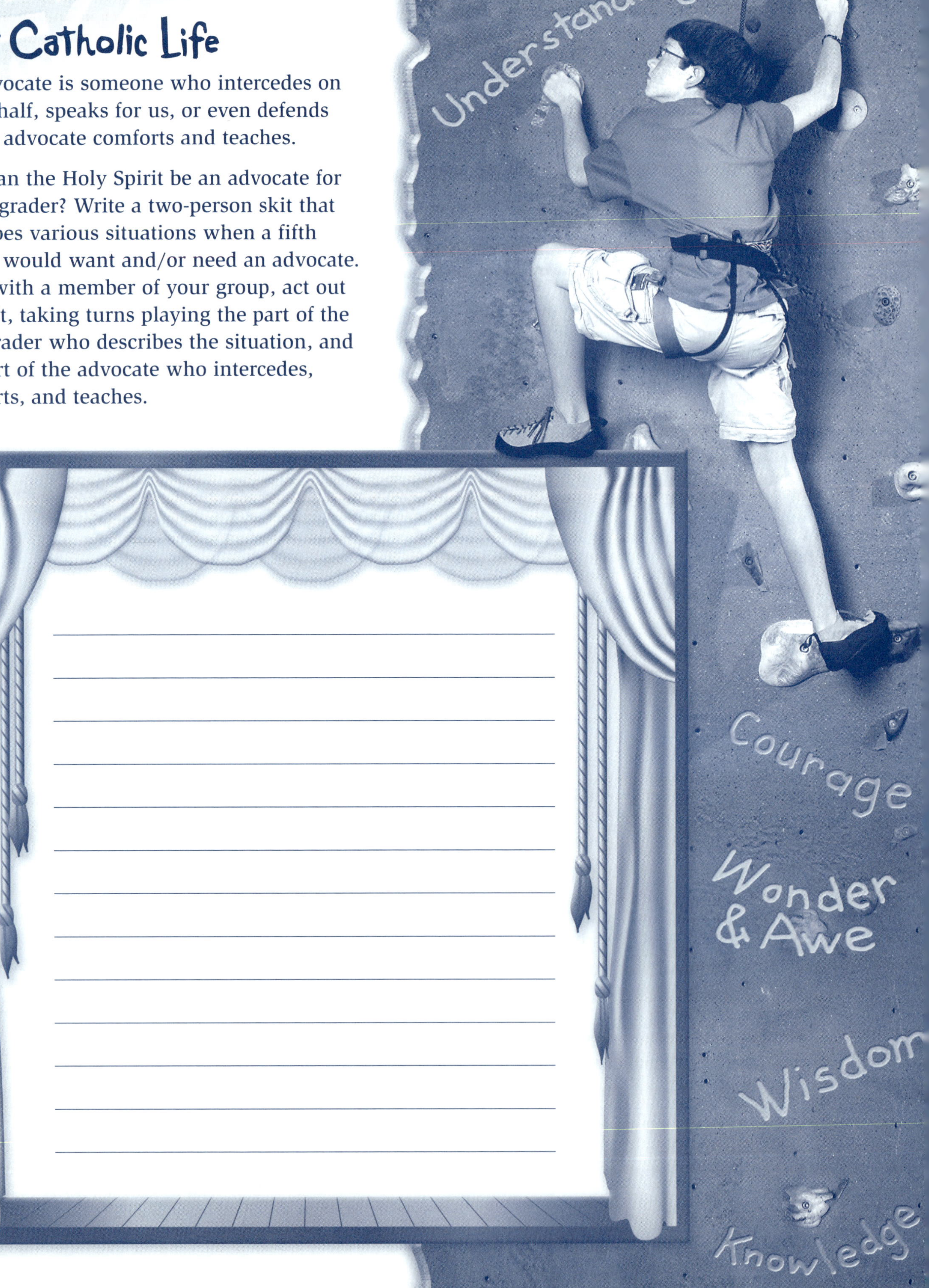

Jesus Christ, the Bread of Life

Remember

At the Last Supper Jesus gave us the gift of himself and instituted the Eucharist. Through the Eucharist, Jesus remains with us forever. In the Eucharist, we honor Jesus by remembering what he did for us, share in a meal, and participate in a sacrifice.

Write why the Eucharist is a memorial, a meal, and a sacrifice.

Key Words

Unscramble these words. Then write the correct word to complete the sentences.

S E O V A R S P

___ ___ ___ ___ ___ ___ ___ ___

S U I C A R E T H

___ ___ ___ ___ ___ ___ ___ ___ ___

C I R A I C S E F

___ ___ ___ ___ ___ ___ ___ ___ ___

E E C P E N R S

___ ___ ___ ___ ___ ___ ___ ___

A ______________________________
is a gift offered to God by a priest in the name of all the people.

The______________________________
is the sacrament of the Body and Blood of Christ. It is the only sacrament of initiation that we receive again and again.

The real ________________________
means that Jesus is really and truly present in the Eucharist.

The feast on which Jewish people remember the miraculous way that God saved them from death and slavery in ancient Egypt is called ____________________________.

Reflect & Pray

Choose one of the gospel passages from this chapter's "We Gather in Prayer" to learn by heart. Work with a family member or friend. Recite the passage several times as your partner checks your progress.

Once you have memorized the passage, write about your experience.

The passage I chose is

____

______________________________.

The reason I chose this passage is

____

______________________________.

I will remember this passage when

____

______________________________.

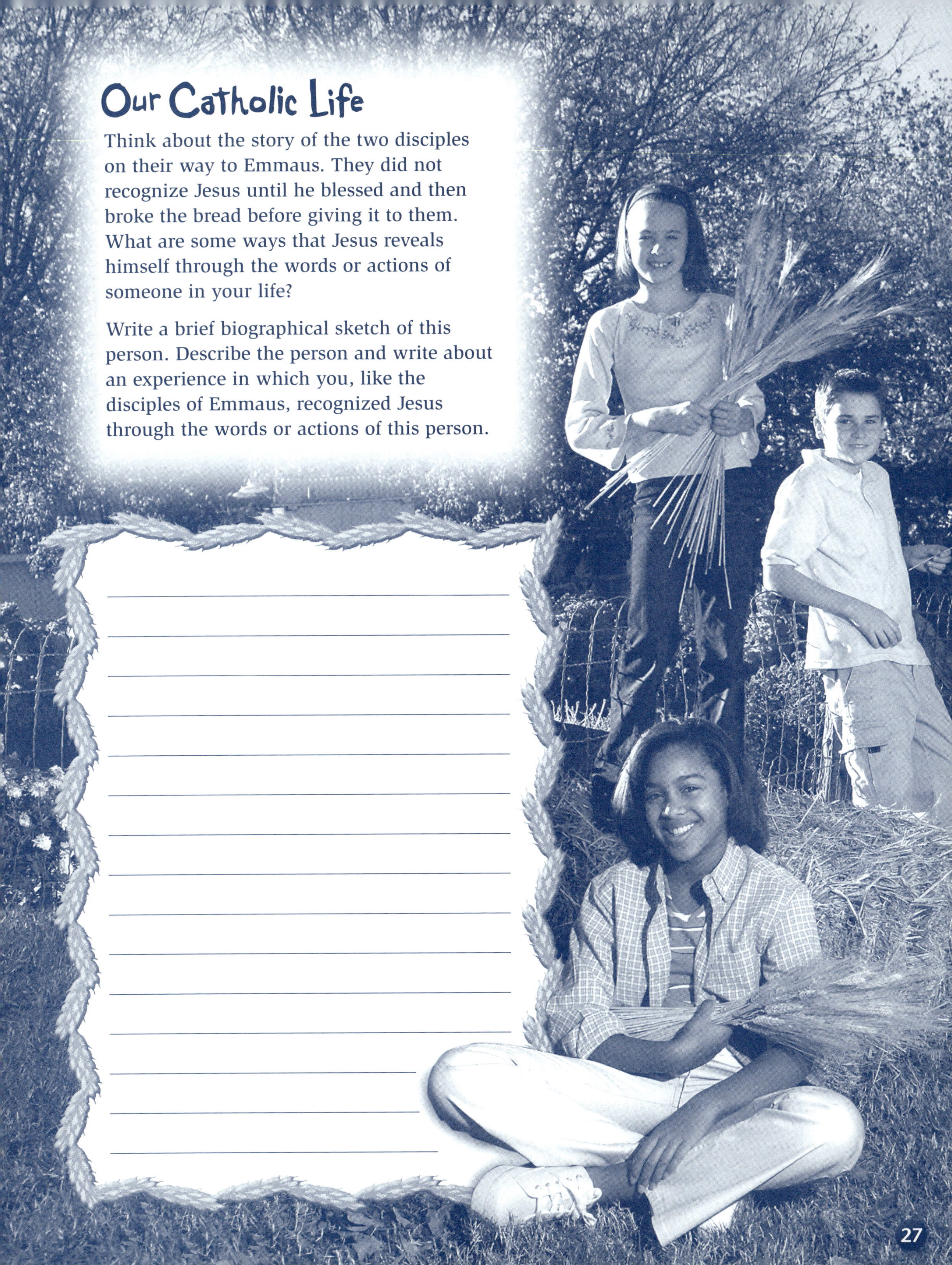

Our Catholic Life

Think about the story of the two disciples on their way to Emmaus. They did not recognize Jesus until he blessed and then broke the bread before giving it to them. What are some ways that Jesus reveals himself through the words or actions of someone in your life?

Write a brief biographical sketch of this person. Describe the person and write about an experience in which you, like the disciples of Emmaus, recognized Jesus through the words or actions of this person.

The Celebration of the Eucharist

Remember

The Mass is another name for the celebration of the Eucharist. The assembly, or community of people gathered to worship in the name of Jesus, participates in many ways throughout the Mass.

There are many people who help us during the celebration. What are some of the roles people play in the Eucharist? Write the letter to match the sentence beginning to the correct sentence ending.

a. The presider is the priest who

b. The deacon has a special role in

c. Special ministers of the Eucharist help to

d. Greeters or ushers often

e. Musicians help the whole assembly to

____ distribute Holy Communion.

____ welcome us before Mass begins.

____ does and says the things Jesus did at the Last Supper.

____ participate in Mass through song.

____ proclaiming the gospel and in the preaching.

Key Words

Each description tells something about one of the *Key Words*. Write the correct word after each clue. Then draw a picture to show what we do during one part of the Mass.

In this part of the Mass, we are united as a community.

____

In this part of the Mass, we listen and respond to God's word.

____

In this part of the Mass, the death and Resurrection of Christ are made present again.

____

In this part of the eucharistic prayer, the bread and wine become the Body and Blood of Christ.

____

In this part of the Mass, we are blessed and sent forth to be Christ's servants in the world.

____

Reflect & Pray

The Concluding Rite at Mass sends us out to be the Body of Christ to others.

Write a song or special beat that we can sing during the Concluding Rite.

Our Catholic Life

We work at being the Body of Christ when we share our gifts and talents.

What gifts do you have to share with others? Your gift may be a special talent that makes others happy. You may have the gift of time or friendship. Write the special gifts you have to offer and write what you can do to share these gifts.

Living As Prayerful People

Remember

In prayer we open our hearts and minds to God. God calls to us in prayer, and we respond. Jesus taught us to pray with patience and complete trust in God.

How would you teach someone about prayer? Design a handbook to help people who may not know much about prayer. Title one page "Kinds of Prayer," and another page "Places to Pray." Write under each heading information and practical tips to help people to pray. Share the handbook with a friend or family member. Note what they found helpful and if they think anything else should be included.

Kinds of Prayer

____

____

____

____

____

____

____

____

____

Places to Pray

____

____

____

____

____

____

____

____

____

Key Words

Use each of the *Key Words* in a sentence.

holy day of obligation

____
____
____

sacramentals

____
____
____

Liturgy of the Hours

____
____
____

Reflect & Pray

The habit of daily prayer grows by making special times for prayer. We can pray in the morning and offer our entire day to God. We can give thanks to God for his many gifts both before and after meals. We can pray at night as we think about ways we have or have not shown love for God and for others.

Think about other activities that you do each day, such as doing the dishes or caring for a pet. In the space, draw yourself doing the activity and write a prayer to go with this activity. Copy the prayer onto a card and post it in a place where you will see it each time you do this activity.

Our Catholic Life

How much do you share in the rich Catholic tradition of special practices and popular devotions? Ask a family member or friend to help you answer the following questions.

Q. What is the Exposition of the Blessed Sacrament?

A. ______________________________

____

Q. What happens during the ceremony called Benediction?

A. ______________________________

____

Q. What are novenas?

A. ______________________________

____

Q. What is the purpose of the stations of the cross?

A. ______________________________

____

Q. What are some popular devotions your family has participated in?

A. ______________________________

____

Q. Where can you find out more about these special practices and popular devotions?

A. ______________________________

____

We Turn to God

Remember

Jesus told the parable of the man with two sons to help us understand what it means to be sorry for our actions and to turn back to God. God is like the forgiving father in this story. Reread the story in your *We Believe* text.

Design a series of billboards depicting the most important points in the story. The billboards will be seen by thousands of travelers. Sketch your ideas in the correct sequence on the billboards.

Unscramble the *Key Words* and complete the sentences.

n c i o a i l R e o n c t i

_ _ _ _ _ _ _ _ _ _ _ _ _ _

n v c o e s n r i o

_ _ _ _ _ _ _ _ _ _

i n s

_ _ _

__________________ is a turning to God with all one's heart.

In the sacrament of __________________, our relationship with God and the Church is strengthened or restored and our sins are forgiven.

A __________________ is a thought, word, deed or omission against God's law.

Reflect & Pray

Look at the song "We Belong to God's Family" in your *We Believe* text. With a family member or friend, plan a video to go along with the song. Use this video storyboard.

Our Catholic Life

Paolo and Ben were working together on their International Day project on the country of Argentina. They went to the library and gathered facts for their poster. Paolo, with the help of his mother, would bring in a special dish of the country. Ben, with the help of his father, would make a plaster relief map.

On the morning of International Day, Paolo came to school without the special dish. Paolo apologized and said, "I'm really sorry, Ben. My mom got home late from work. We didn't have time to prepare the food for today." Ben was angry and said, "You've ruined the whole project! Now we'll both get a bad grade because of you!"

What do you think will happen next? Use the following questions to help guide you as you finish the story.

- How does each of the boys feel?
- How does this disagreement affect their friends, family, and classmates?
- What will each of them need to do in order to reconcile with each other?
- How will others be affected by their reconciliation?

____

____

____

____

____

____

____

____

____

____

____

____

The Celebration of Reconciliation

Remember

The sacrament of Reconciliation strengthens or restores our relationship with God and others, and our sins are forgiven. In this sacrament, the Church celebrates God's forgiveness, and we trust in his mercy.

How would you respond to this e-mail from a friend? Write your response.

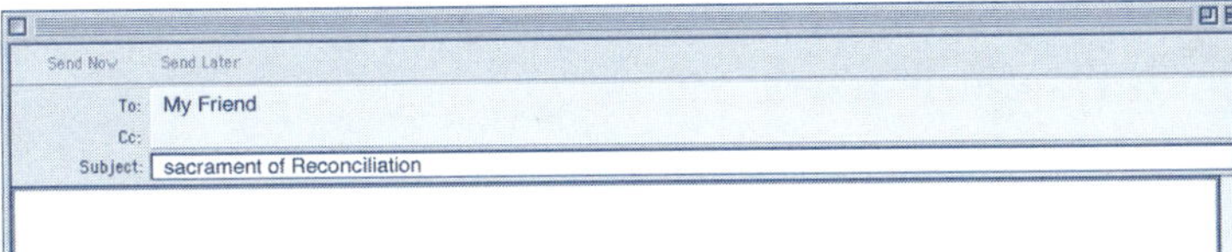

Dear Friend,

I am trying to learn more about the sacrament of Reconciliation. I know that it includes four major parts. Could you tell me one thing about each part? Thank you so much!

Send Now Send Later

To: My Friend

Cc:

Subject: Re: sacrament of Reconciliation

____

____

____

____

____

____

____

____

____

____

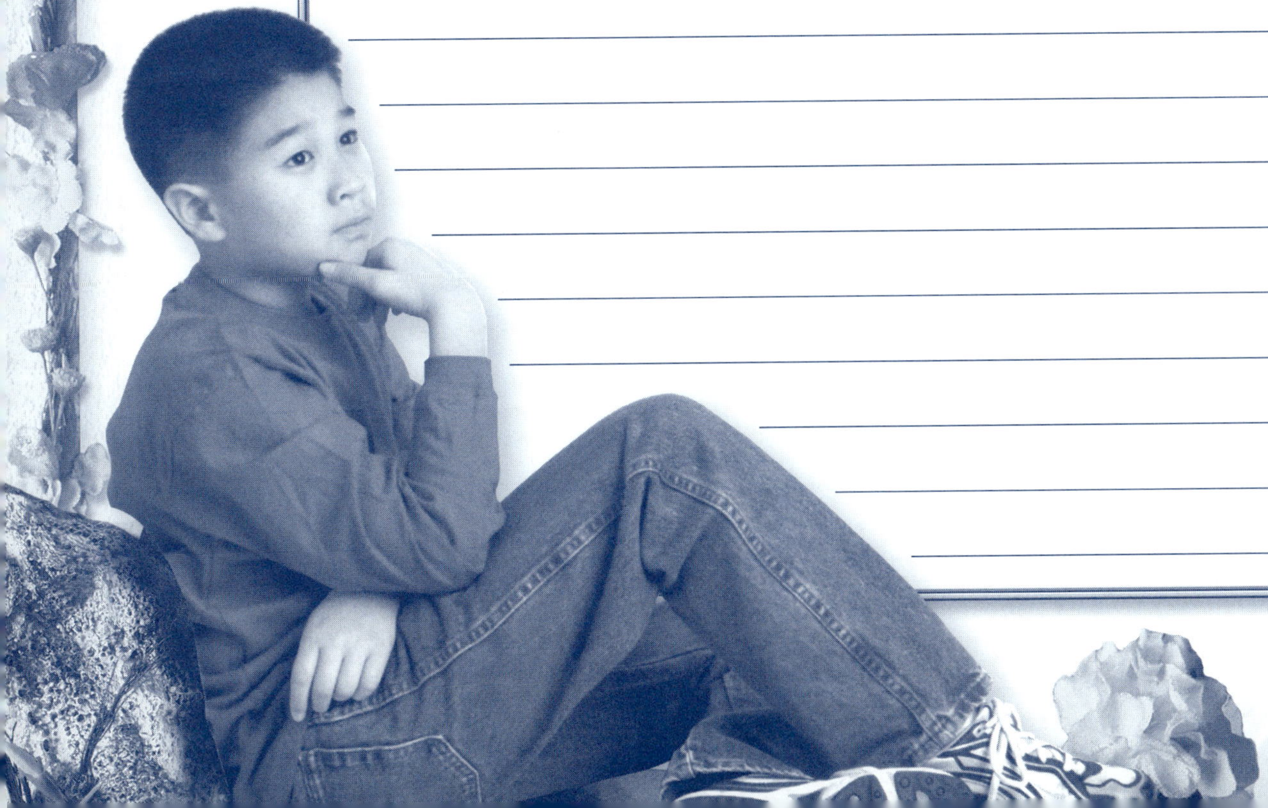

Our conscience is the ability to know the difference between good and evil, right and wrong.

Write a public service announcement that will encourage others to examine their conscience. Explain what happens when we examine our conscience. Use *conscience* at least three times and circle it each time it is used.

Reflect & Pray

An act of contrition is a prayer that allows us to express our sorrow and promise to try not to sin again. We can say we are sorry in many ways. Write your own prayer of contrition that includes an expression of sorrow for sin, the asking of forgiveness, and the intent to try not to sin again.

Our Catholic Life

The community of faith helps us to turn our lives to God. With a family member or friend, discuss various communities or groups, such as family, school, and parish.

In the spaces, write a short story or draw a picture that tells how each community or organization helps us to turn our lives to God.

Jesus, the Healer

Remember

Many people grew to believe in Jesus because of his healing actions. Jesus felt great love for those who were suffering, and he healed many of them. Jesus desired to heal people from sin, too. Often when he cured the sick, he also forgave their sins.

With a member of your family or group, write a newspaper interview that describes the healing and forgiving actions of Jesus and what they mean. Include several "quotes" from people who experienced Jesus' forgiveness.

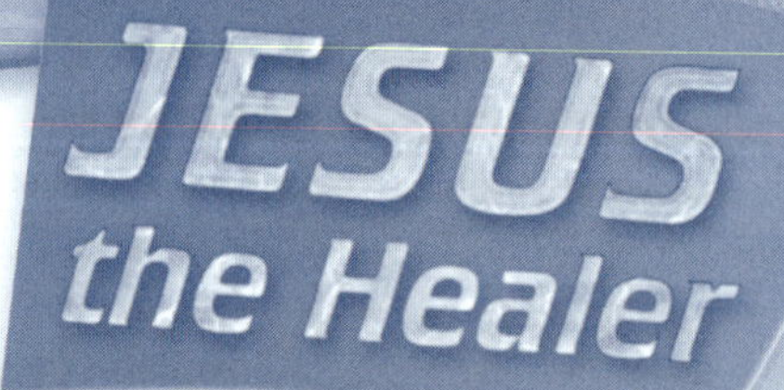

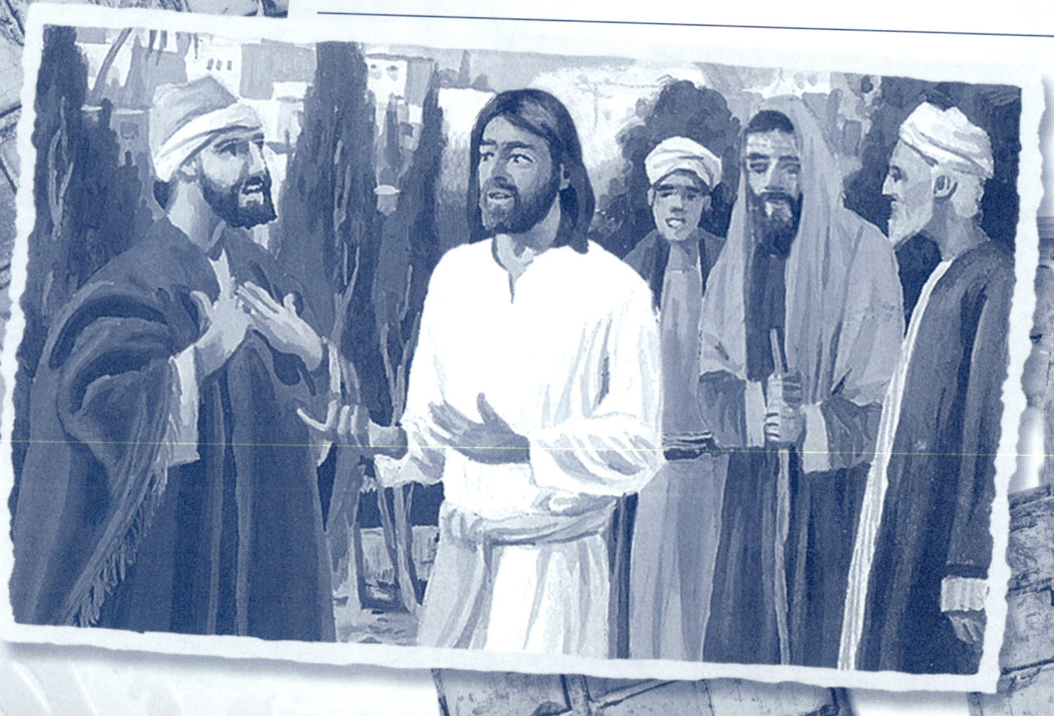

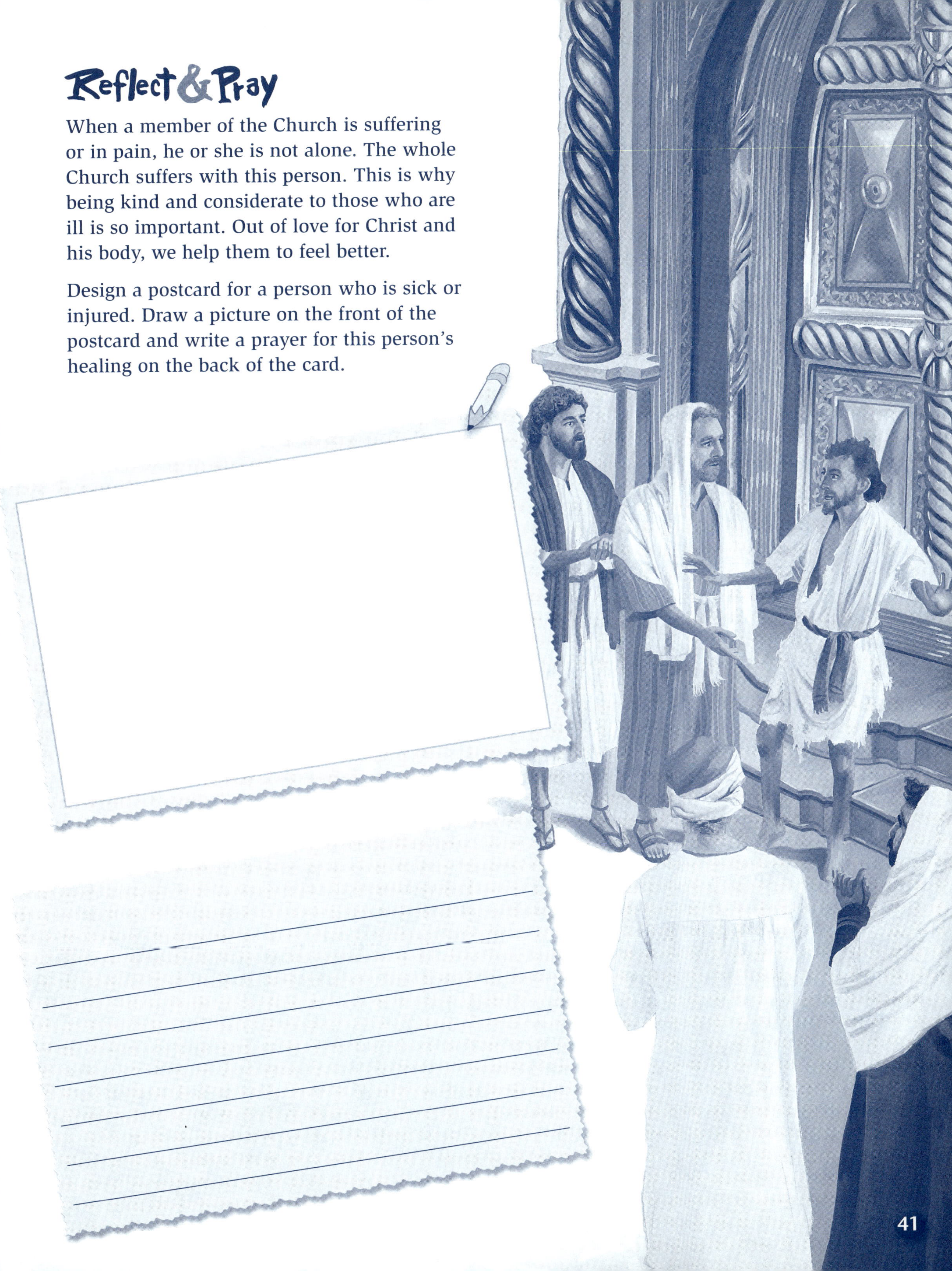

Reflect & Pray

When a member of the Church is suffering or in pain, he or she is not alone. The whole Church suffers with this person. This is why being kind and considerate to those who are ill is so important. Out of love for Christ and his body, we help them to feel better.

Design a postcard for a person who is sick or injured. Draw a picture on the front of the postcard and write a prayer for this person's healing on the back of the card.

Test your knowledge about the sacrament of the Anointing of the Sick. Circle True or False. Then change any false statements to make them true.

True or False   In this sacrament, God's grace and comfort are given to those who are seriously ill or suffering because of their old age.

____

____

True or False   The sacrament of the Anointing of the Sick is a sacrament of initiation.

____

____

True or False   Those who celebrate this sacrament receive strength, peace, and courage to face the difficulties that come from serious illness.

____

____

True or False   This sacrament celebrates, in a special way, Jesus' missionary work.

____

____

Our Catholic Life

All who are baptized are joined together in the Body of Christ. What happens to one member affects us all. The whole Church remembers in prayer those who are sick, especially when we gather at Sunday Mass. We pray for the strength and healing of those who are sick in the general intercessions of the Mass.

With a member of your family or group, find out what else a parish does to care for the sick. What roles do various people and committees in the parish play? Check your parish Web site or bulletin to learn what the parish does to reach out to those who are sick or elderly. List your ideas about other ways your parish could help those who are sick.

The Celebration of the Anointing of the Sick

God always remembers those who are sick and suffering. We believe that when we are suffering, Jesus is with us sharing in our pain. In the sacrament of the Anointing of the Sick, Christ comforts those who are sick and he suffers with them. The Anointing of the Sick continues Jesus' saving work of healing.

Like all sacraments, the Anointing of the Sick is a celebration of the whole community of the faithful. The main parts of this sacrament are the:

- prayer of faith
- laying on of hands
- anointing with oil.

In the frames, illustrate what happens in each of these three main parts. Then describe the importance of each part.

Reflect & Pray

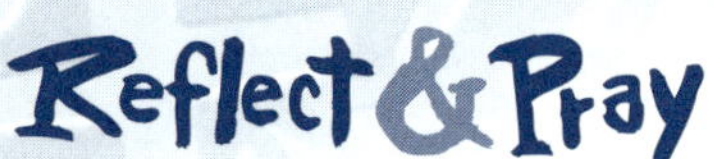

The prayer of faith has been an important part of the Church's celebration of the sacrament from the beginning of the Church. The whole Church is represented by the priest, family, friends, and parish members gathered to pray. Trusting in God's mercy, they offer several intentions and ask for help for those who are sick.

Work with a member of your family or group. Write several prayers of intention for people who are emotionally or physically sick. Write your prayer, and then offer it with others in your group or in your family.

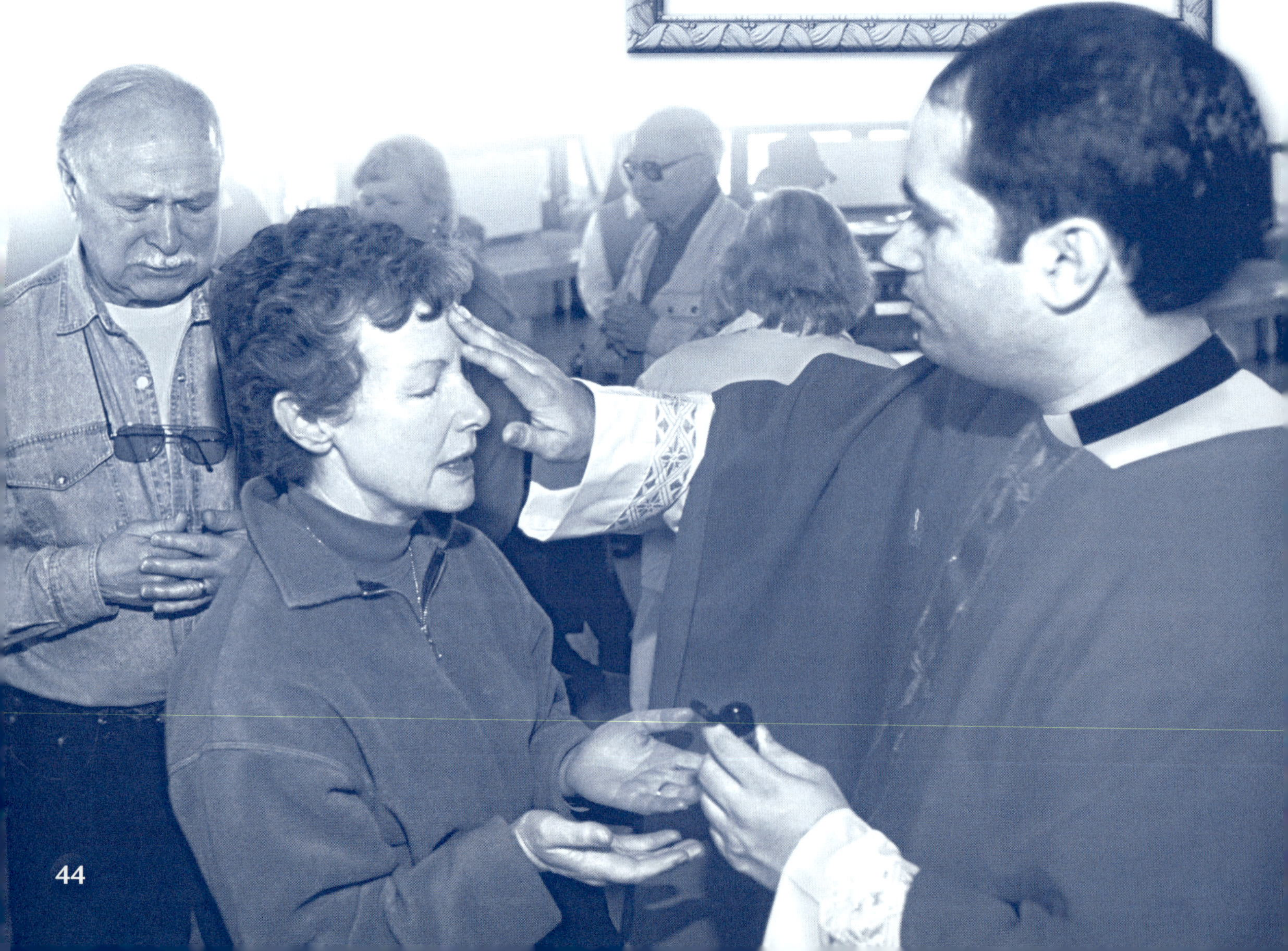

Our Catholic Life

At one time or another in our lives, we will probably get sick. During these times, we may become lonely or worried. We may even wonder if God remembers us. Yet God always remembers those who are sick and suffering. Our care for those who are suffering around the world helps us to grow closer to Jesus.

Write a movie script about someone who is sick. Give your character a name and describe his or her situation. Write about ways others help care for this person. Use dialogue to show what the characters are saying to each other. Give your script an appropriate title.

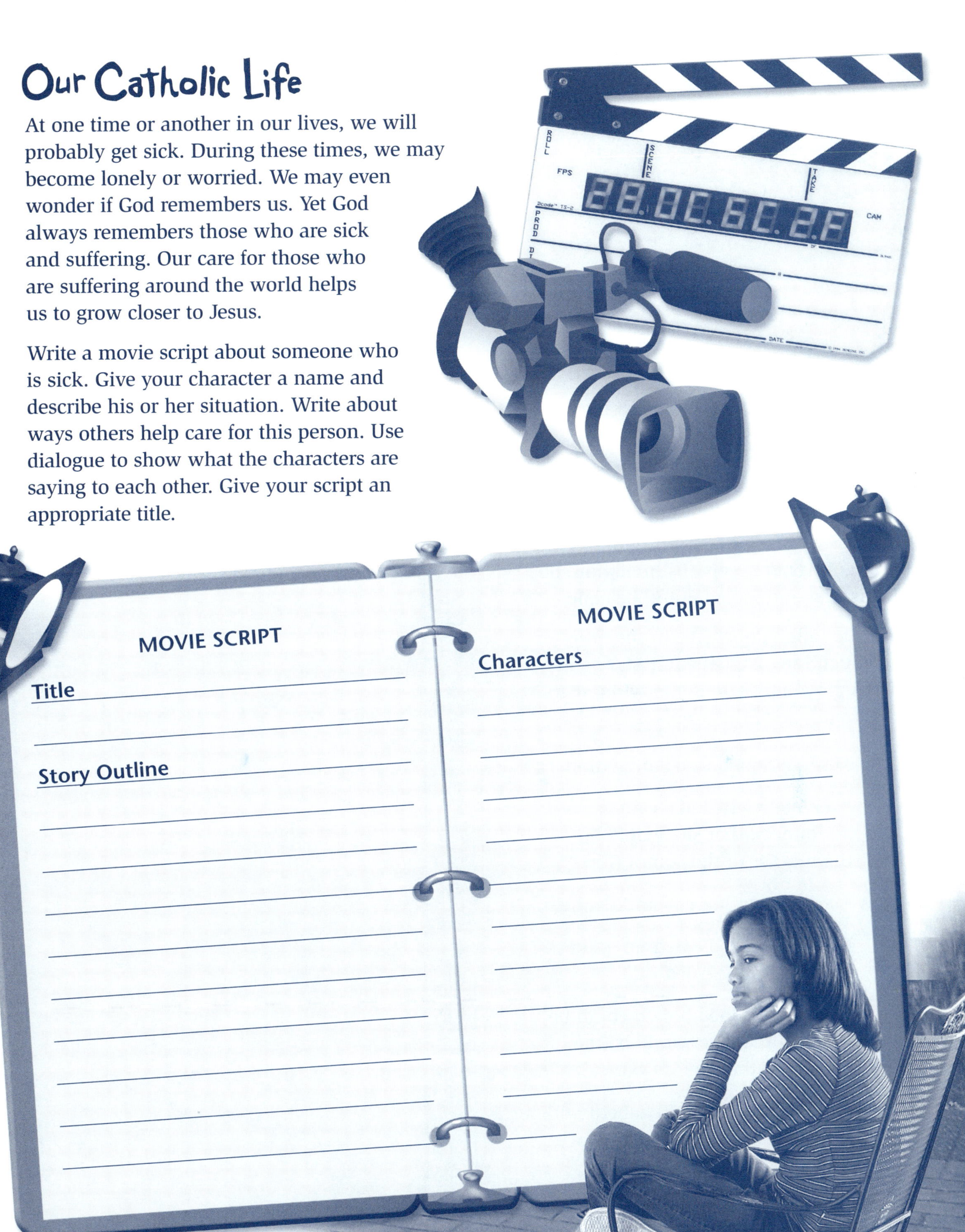

Mary, Model of Discipleship

Remember

Mary was chosen by God from among all the women of history to be the mother of his Son. Mary's faith and love for God brought her to accept his invitation. She is his first and most faithful disciple.

Put the following events in the order in which they happened in Mary's life. Then draw a picture in the window to illustrate one of the events.

____ Mary accepted God's invitation.

____ An angel visited Mary and announced that she would be the mother of the Son of God.

____ Mary visited her cousin Elizabeth.

____ Mary loved and cared for Jesus as he grew and learned.

____ Mary questioned how it could be possible that she would be the mother of the Son of God.

____ Mary responded to Elizabeth with a song called the Canticle of Mary.

Key Words

Unscramble the words. Use these words to complete the paragraph.

U N A O N I N N T I A C

_ _ _ _ _ _ _ _ _ _ _ _

P I T A N O S M S U

_ _ _ _ _ _ _ _ _ _

M L T I U A E A C M

_ _ _ _ _ _ _ _ _ _

We first learn about Mary at the ______________________ which is the name given to the angel's visit to Mary. The angel announced that Mary would be the mother of the Son of God. Mary was blessed by God. She was free from original sin from the moment she was conceived. This belief is called the ____________________ Conception. We believe that when Mary's work on earth was done, God brought her body and soul to live forever with the risen Christ. This belief is called the ______________________.

Reflect & Pray

Catholics all over the world honor Mary through prayer. We ask Mary to pray for us and to speak to her son on our behalf in prayers of intercession. To intercede means to "ask on behalf of."

Look through the newspaper, or look at a news report on television or the Internet. What are some local or global problems in the news? Write a prayer of intercession asking Mary for her prayers.

____

____

____

____

____

____

____

____

____

Our Catholic Life

Interviews help us get to know someone. We can learn from an interviewer's questions and from the person's responses.

What questions would you ask Mary in an interview? How might she respond to your questions? Write interview questions for Mary. Then with a family member or partner write the answers Mary might respond.

Faith, Hope, and Love

CHAPTER 22 REVIEW & RESOURCE

Remember

The theological virtues of faith, hope, and love bring us closer to God and increase our desire to be with God forever.

Every day we have the opportunity to make choices. Sometimes we may not even realize it, but these choices show whether or not we follow Jesus' example. Write about ways in which you can make daily choices to allow faith, hope, and love to bring you closer to God.

Faith brings me closer to God when I …

Hope brings me closer to God when I …

Love brings me closer to God when I …

Reflect & Pray

Hope is a gift that helps us to respond to the happiness that God offers us now and in the future. Think about what makes you happy now, such as listening to music or enjoying sports with friends. Think about things you hope will give you happiness in the future. Draw some here. Pray quietly telling God about your hopes for the future.

Key Words

Complete each sentence by writing the correct *Key Word*. Then write a poem about one or two of these words.

________________ helps us to believe in God and all that the Church has to teach us.

________________ makes us confident in God's love and care for us.

________________ is a good habit that helps us act according to God's love for us.

________________ is the greatest of all virtues. It is the goal of our lives as Christians.

Our Catholic Life

What saints are models for you of living the life of virtue? List their names here.

Choose one of these saints. In books of saints, or on the Internet, find out more about the saint's life. Write an outline for a documentary about the saint.

Called to Live as Jesus' Disciples

Remember

Jesus calls the baptized to serve him in the priesthood of the faithful. As members of the priesthood of the faithful, we continue to learn about Jesus and the teachings of the Church. Each and every one of us is called to worship God, spread the good news of Jesus Christ, and serve one another and the Church.

With a family or group member, write three *For Your Information* cards. Describe how a fifth-grader can share in Christ's priestly mission by:

- worshiping
- serving others
- sharing God's word.

Decorate the borders of each card.

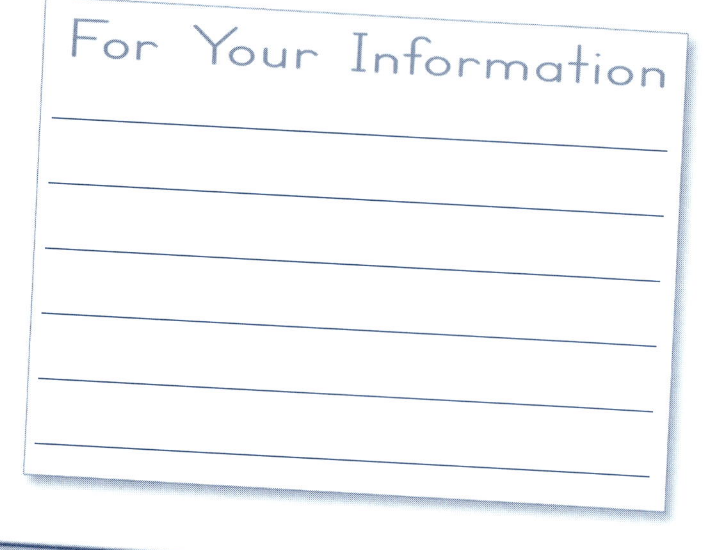

Key Words

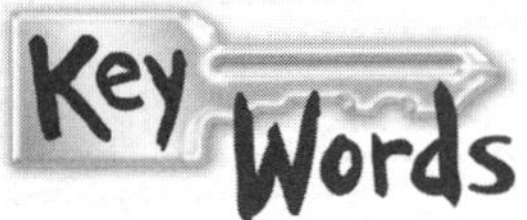

priesthood of the faithful

laypeople

religious

Write a brief Public Service Announcement that includes important information about each of the *Key Words*. Make sure that you tell what is important about each word and why it is important.

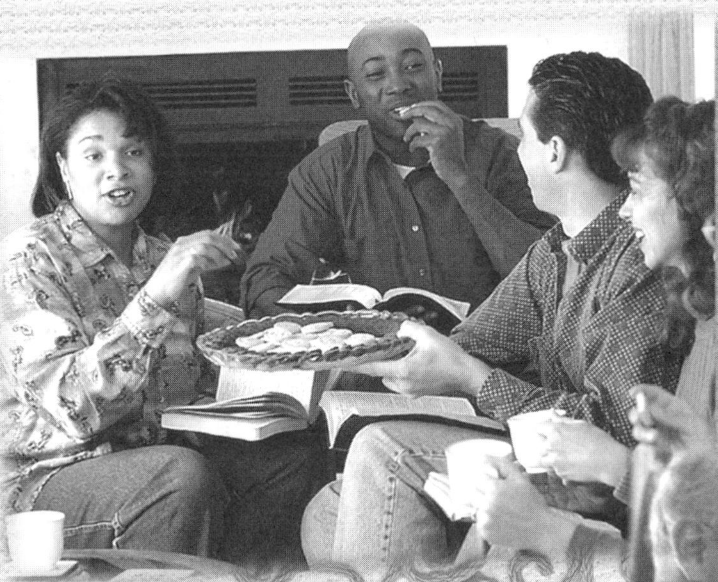

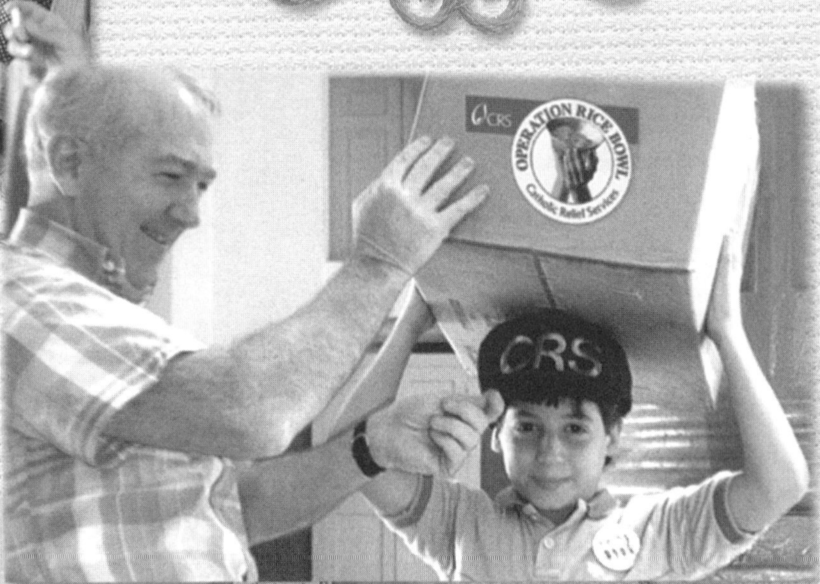

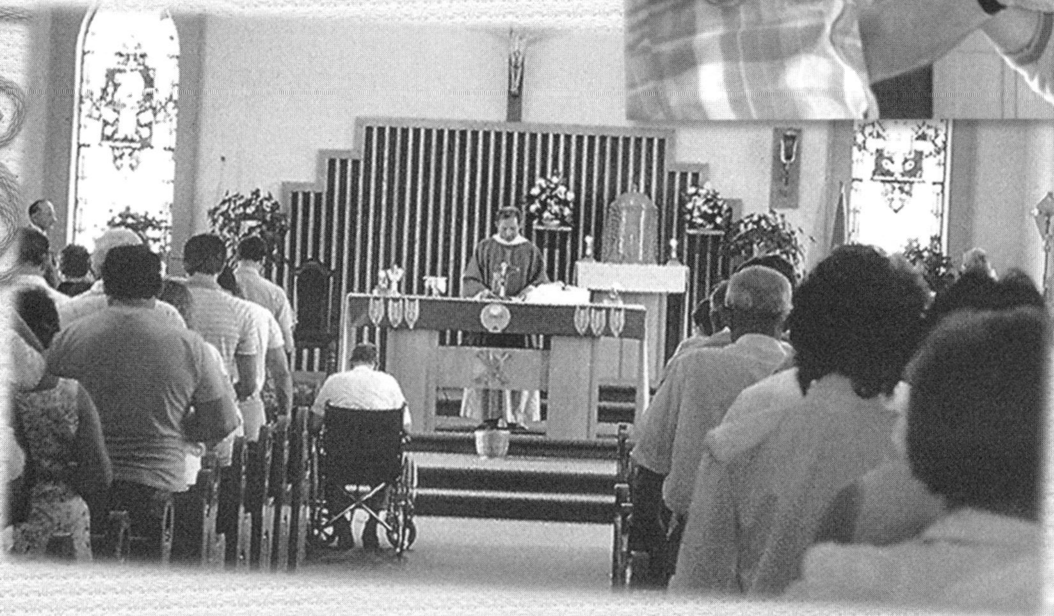

Reflect & Pray

The laity share in the mission to bring the good news of Christ to the world. They share God's love in their families and parishes and live as an example of Christian living for others. Write a prayer of thanksgiving for the laity of the Church.

Our Catholic Life

Friendships are an important part of finding out what it means to be faithful to Christ and one another. Through our friendships we learn what it means to be true to each other, to be honest, and to keep promises.

Complete the following activity with someone from your family or group.

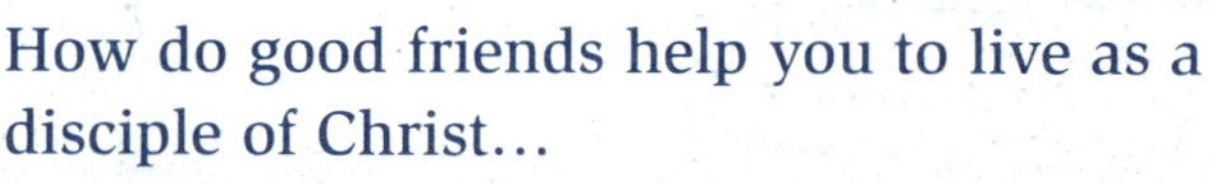

How do good friends help you to live as a disciple of Christ…

…in your home?

…in school?

…in your neighborhood?

Matrimony: A Promise of Faithfulness and Love

Remember

Marriage was part of God's plan from the very beginning and is an effective sign of Jesus' love and presence. In the sacrament of Matrimony, a man and woman become husband and wife. With members of the Church community present, a couple's love is blessed and strengthened by the grace of this sacrament.

What ways can a couple live out the promises of Matrimony? Complete the following sentences.

- A couple promises to ____________ and be ____________________ to each other always.
- A couple lovingly ______________ their children as a ______________ from God.
- A couple is strengthened by God's ____________________ to live out their ____________________ to Christ and each other.

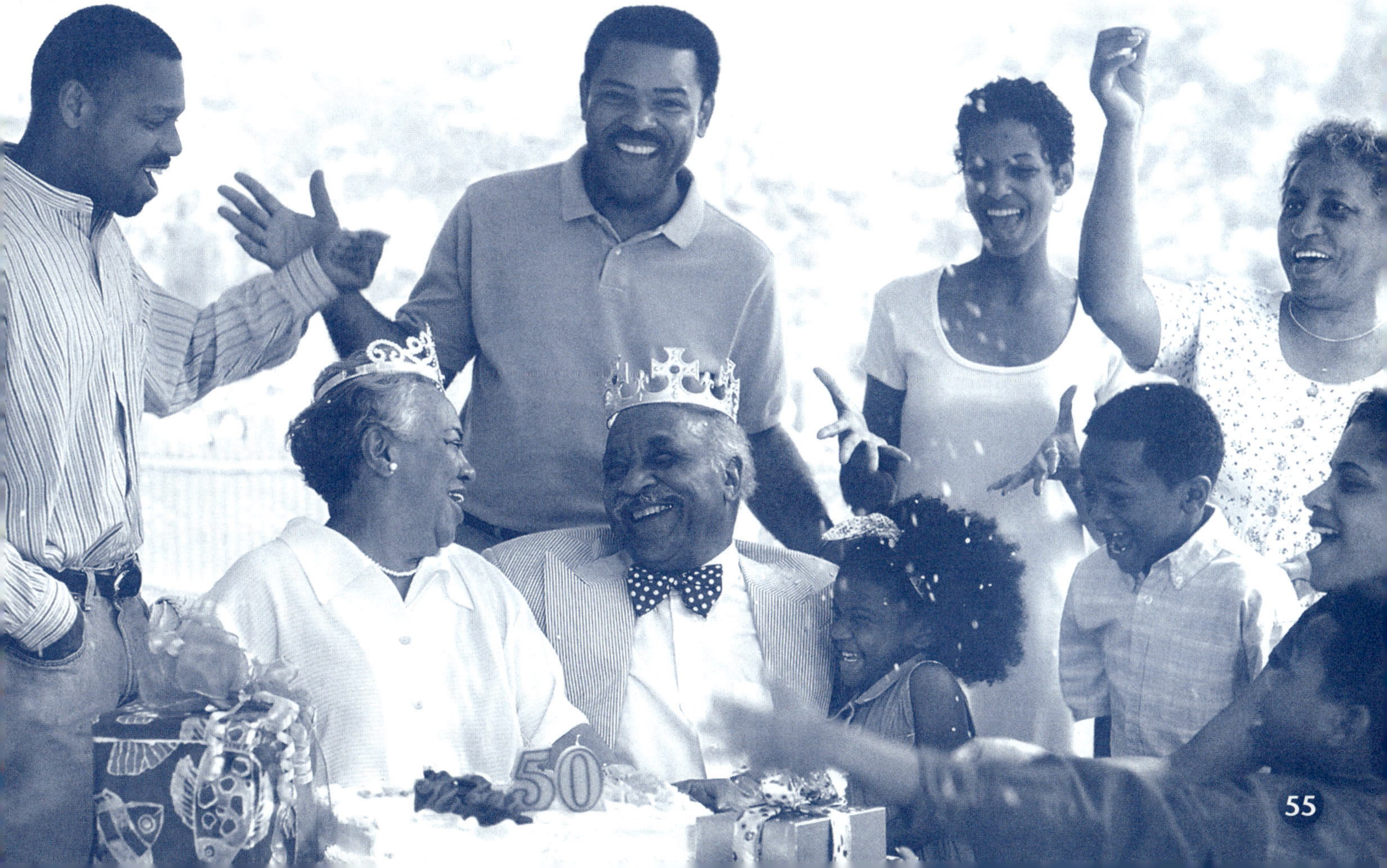

Key Words

Imagine your cousin is getting married. Write a note to tell your cousin what you know about the marriage covenant, fidelity, and the sacrament of Matrimony.

Reflect & Pray

Read the following blessing prayer. With a member of your family or group, make up gestures to go with each line of the blessing. Offer the prayer with a partner.

May the God of hope fill us
with every joy in believing.
May the peace of Christ
abound in our hearts.
May the Holy Spirit
enrich us with his gifts,
now and for ever.
Amen.

Our Catholic Life

Being part of a family means having duties and responsibilities. Write a skit in which a parent or guardian and a child are having a discussion about what it means to be part of a family. Include questions that each may have about his or her duties and responsibilities. Also include ways these duties and responsibilities may be carried out at home, in the parish, neighborhood, and other places.

Holy Orders: A Promise of Service for the People of God

Remember

Jesus sent his apostles out to all parts of the world to lead his community and to bring people to share in his kingdom. The pope, bishops, priests, and deacons continue this work by serving the Church in different ways.

Write a description of three ways bishops, priests, and deacons serve the Church.

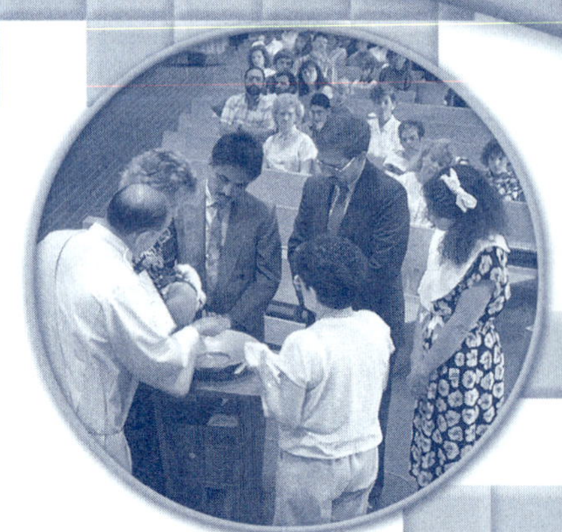

Bishop 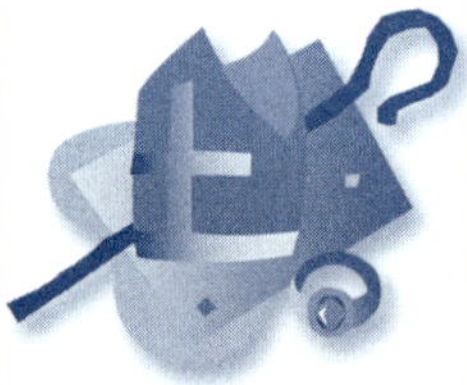	
Priest 	
Deacon 	

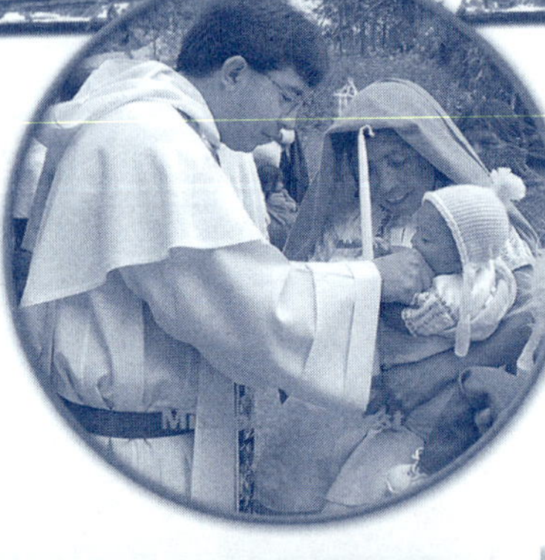

The *Key Words* are hidden in the puzzle. Circle them.

R	T	M	N	O	T	A	P	L	I	P	T
W	X	C	E	E	Y	F	H	G	R	R	G
M	N	P	I	J	H	G	T	R	C	I	V
C	B	D	F	E	H	A	R	C	K	E	B
V	I	M	J	D	E	A	C	O	N	S	K
M	S	U	I	T	S	R	F	P	L	T	N
L	H	O	L	Y	O	R	D	E	R	S	P
D	O	E	Y	H	P	S	T	I	E	N	M
C	P	N	M	U	J	R	S	P	L	J	U
B	S	R	T	P	I	E	R	C	T	R	M
V	B	T	H	K	U	Y	R	G	H	K	O
G	R	D	E	T	J	U	T	E	E	B	L

Write the meaning of each word.

Holy Orders

bishops

priests

deacons

Reflect & Pray

Priests serve by leading, teaching, and most especially celebrating the Eucharist and other sacraments. Write a prayer for priests asking God to strengthen them in their work. Include a special prayer for a specific priest, such as the pastor who serves your parish community.

Our Catholic Life

Holy Orders is the sacrament through which the Church continues the apostles' mission. It is a sacrament of service to others in which men are ordained to serve the Church as deacons, priests, and bishops.

With a family or group member, write a song, poem, or short story describing how priests, deacons, and bishops live out the call to service.

One, Holy, Catholic, and Apostolic

Remember

One, holy, catholic, and apostolic are the four characteristics, or marks of the Church. These are qualities or characteristics that describe the Church and also lead us to unity and holiness, and inspire us to spread God's word.

Complete the following chart. Describe what each mark means in the second column. Design an emblem or logo that symbolizes each characteristic in the third column.

Marks of the Church	Meaning	Emblem or Logo
One		
Holy		
Catholic		
Apostolic		

Reflect & Pray

We respect the rights of others to practice and live their faith in different ways. The work to promote the unity of all Christians is called ecumenism.

Write a prayer for the unity of all Christians and people of faith.

Key Words

Respond to the following statements about the *Key Words* by writing True or False.

______ The first mark is that the Church is one because all its members believe in the one Lord, Jesus Christ.

______ The Church is catholic, or universal, but is not made up of people from all over the world.

______ Christ shares God's holiness with us today through the Church.

______ The Church is apostolic because it is built on the faith of the bishops.

______ The work to promote the unity of some Christians is called ecumenism.

______ Stewards of creation take care of everything that God has given them.

Rewrite any false statements to make them true.

Our Catholic Life

Justice means respect for the rights of others. It also means that we share the resources that come from God's creation with those who do not have them and use the resources we have in a responsible way.

Work with a family or group member to name a solution to the problem in each story. Write your solution on the line.

Your friend Vincent lives in an apartment building with poor lighting in the hallways and missing fire escapes. His family is worried about these unsafe conditions but are not sure what they should do. How could you help them?

Walking home one afternoon you see a younger student being called names by some of her classmates. What could you do to help her?

Your family is having a picnic at the lake. You see that another family leaves without throwing away their paper plates and cups. What should you do?

Vice President Publications, Sadlier
Rosemary K. Calicchio

Executive Director of Catechetics
Carole M. Eipers, D.Min.

Director of Research and Planning
Melissa D. Gibbons

Product Developer
Lee Hlavacek

Editorial Director
Blake Bergen

Supervising Editor
Mary Ann Trevaskiss

Senior Editor
Maureen Gallo

Vice President, Publishing Operations
Deborah Jones

Creative Director
Vince Gallo

Photo Editor
Jim Saylor

Photo Credits
Cover Photography: Ken Karp: *anointing oil & children reading;* PictureQuest/Digital Vision: *ivy vine;* Solus Images/Brian Fraunfelter: *water splash.* Jane Bernard: 11 *bottom left,* 12, 26, 28. Karen Callaway: 11 *top right,* 13 *top,* 20 *bottom left,* 22, 59. Catholic Relief Services/Daniel Medinger: 53 *right.* Comstock Images: 5. Corbis/LWA-Cann Tardiff: 54 *bottom right;* Ariel Skelley: 55. Crosiers/Gene Plaisted, OSC: 11 *top left,* 13 *bottom,* 53 *bottom,* 58 *top,* 60. Neal Farris: 5, 9 *top,* 10, 15, 20 *bottom left,* 21, 24, 27, 33, 35, 36, 37, 38, 39, 42, 45 *bottom,* 48, 49, 61, 63. Getty Images: 13, 16, 26 *background,* 31, 42 *background,* 50, 53 *top,* 54 *top right, middle left & bottom left.* Mark Hayda: 45. Ken Karp: 57. Eugene Llacuna: 29. Materfile/Gary Black: 33 *background.* PictureQuest/Creatas: 10 *background;* IT Stock International/eStock Photography: 18 *top right;* Arthur Tilley/i2i Images: 54 *top left.* The Image Works/Jack Kurtz: 58 *bottom right.* W.P. Wittman Ltd.: 17, 32, 44, 58 *bottom left,* 62.

Illustrator Credits
Cover Design: Kevin Ghiglione. Series Patterned Background Design: Evan Polenghi. Diane Bennett: 58 *icons.* Margaret Chodos-Irvine: 19, 21. Gwen Connelly: 43 *berries/leaves.* Maragret Cusak: 52, 53 *stitched background.* Rob Dunlavey: 8 *food drive.* Suzanne Duranceau: 7. Luigi Galenta: 20. Stephanie Garcia: 37 *rock/flower border.* Janell Genovese: 54 *frame bottom right.* Alex Gross: 51 *saints.* Kate Hosford: 38, 39 *vine/flowers.* W.B. Johnston: 23 *mosaic border,* 46, 47 *faux wood.* Dave LaFleur: 14, 15 *background.* Molly K. Scanlon: 20 *flames,* 24 *curtain,* 30 *gift box,* 34, 39 *church, school, house,* 45, 46 *frame,* 51 *computer.* Kristina Swarner: 6. Andrew Wheatcroft: 4, 25, 40, 41, 47 *scripture art.*